WELCOME TO
UNLOCKING HAPPINESS

YOUR GUIDE TO ACTIVITIES THAT BOOST YOUR MOOD

Embark on a journey to elevate your daily mood and harness the transformative power of happiness. Inside these pages, you'll discover the scientific underpinnings of how activities can significantly boost your well-being and learn why embracing new experiences is key to a fulfilling life.

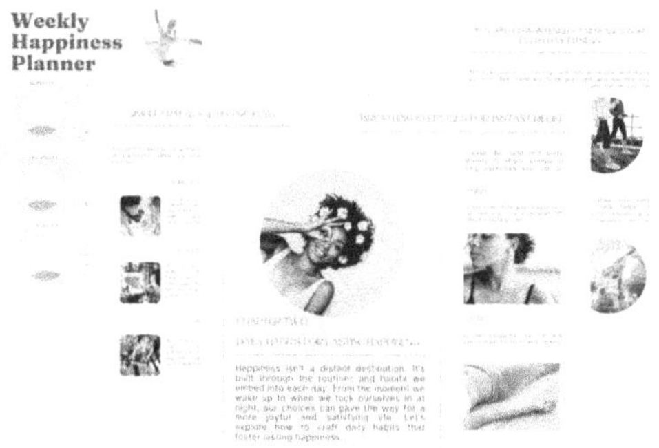

What Will You Gain from This eBook?

- Science-Backed Insights
- Practical Strategies
- Daily Habits
- Inspiring Activties
- Creative and Social Pursuits
- Mindfulness and Relaxation Techniques
- Customizable Planner

Ready to Boost Your Happiness? Start your journey now! Scan the QR code or follow the link below to join our newsletter for exclusive content, and begin building your joyful life today.

Send me my free e-book <u>Unlocking Happiness</u>

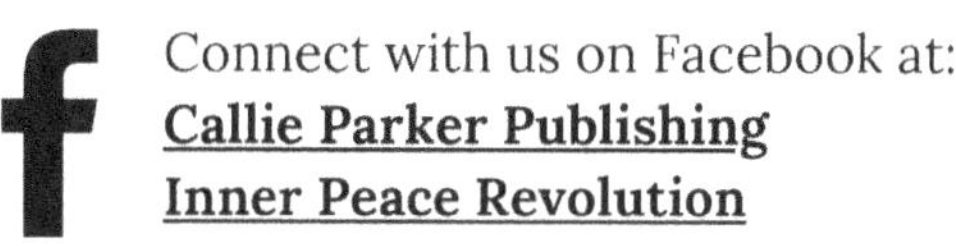

Connect with us on Facebook at:
Callie Parker Publishing
Inner Peace Revolution

THE SHADOW WORK JOURNAL FOR TEENS

Guided Prompts and Activities for Inner Healing, Building Confidence, and Practicing Self-Love

CALLIE PARKER

Guided Journal

Introduction to the Shadow Work Journal for Teens

Welcome to the Shadow Work Journal for Teens, your guide on an extraordinary journey of self-discovery and personal growth. Adolescence is a time of transformation, and this journal is your trusted companion on the exciting journey of uncovering your true self, understanding your hidden aspects, and embracing the power of your shadow. This journal is designed to complement and enhance your experience with the main book, *Shadow Work for Teens: A Guide for Teenagers and Young Adults to Overcome Inner Challenges, Build Confidence, and Practice Self-Love.*

The Purpose of the Journal

The purpose of this journal is simple yet profound—to provide you with a safe and nurturing space to explore the various facets of your personality, emotions, and experiences. It's a tool for diving deep into your own psyche, understanding the dynamics that influence your thoughts and behaviors, and ultimately, fostering a sense of self-acceptance and authenticity. By following along with the main book, you will find this journal to be a practical resource that brings the concepts and exercises to life, helping you integrate what you learn into your daily experiences.

The Importance of Reflection for Teens

Reflection is a vital skill, especially during your teenage years. This period of life is marked by countless changes, from physical development to the exploration of your identity and beliefs. Reflecting on your experiences, emotions, and choices helps you make sense of the world around you and the world within you. It allows you to grow, adapt, and make informed decisions as you navigate the exciting and sometimes challenging path to adulthood. This journal, in conjunction with the main book, provides a structured way to engage in this reflective practice, ensuring that you get the most out of your shadow work journey.

Using This Journal

Using this journal is both simple and rewarding. Here's a brief guide to help you get started:

1. Create a Quiet Space: Find a peaceful and private place where you can write without distractions. It could be a cozy corner of your room, a park bench, or a quiet cafe.
2. Set Aside Time: Dedicate regular time for journaling. Whether it's in the morning, before bed, or during breaks, consistency is key to making the most of this experience.
3. Express Yourself: There are no right or wrong answers here. This journal is all about your unique journey. Write honestly, without judgment. Let your thoughts flow freely.
4. Engage with the Prompts: Each chapter presents prompts and exercises tailored to specific aspects of shadow work. Use these prompts as a starting point for reflection and self-exploration.
5. Embrace the Journey: Remember that this is a process, not a destination. Embrace your shadows, acknowledge your strengths, and be compassionate with yourself along the way.
6. Use Additional Tools: Feel free to use art, doodles, or any creative expression to supplement your journaling. Your journal is your canvas.
7. Revisit and Reflect: As you progress, revisit your earlier entries and reflect on how you've grown and changed. It's a testament to your journey.

The pages of this journal are waiting to be filled with your thoughts, feelings, and discoveries. It's an invitation to embark on an inward adventure, to understand your shadow, and to shine a light on the unique and beautiful person you are becoming. Embrace this journey with an open heart, and you'll find that the path to self-discovery is an exciting and empowering one.

Table of Contents

The Unconscious

THE UNCONSCIOUS MIND

Describe a dream you've had recently. What emotions or symbols were present?

Reflect on a habit or behavior you can't explain. How might it be related to your unconscious mind?

Write about a memory from your childhood that still affects your emotions. What do you think it reveals about your unconscious?

Explore a fear or phobia you have. What could be its roots in your unconscious?

How do you feel about the idea of exploring your unconscious mind through shadow work? Write about any apprehensions or excitement.

Start a dream journal and record your dreams regularly. Analyze recurring symbols or themes.

Try a guided meditation or mindfulness exercise to connect with your unconscious thoughts and feelings.

Create an artwork or visual representation of a recent dream or a vivid memory that relates to your unconscious.

Date: _______________________

Title or Brief Description

Dream Details

Describe the dream in as much detail as you can recall. Note the environment, characters, objects, colors and emotions you felt during the dream.

Potential Triggers

Were there any events or experiences from the day before that might have influenced this dream?

Recurring Elements

Are there elements in this dream that have appeared in previous dreams? If yes, jot them down.

Date: _______________

Emotional Resonance

How did the dream make you feel upon waking? Was there a particular emotion that stood out?

Symbols and Significance

Are there symbols, themes or motifs in the dream that relate to you as a teen? Reflect on their potential significance.

Desires and Fears

Did the dream reveal any hidden desires or fears? How do they relate to your waking life?

Messages from the Unconscious

Sometimes dreams carry messages or insights from our unconscious mind. Do you feel there's a message in this dream for you?

Date: _______________________

Dreams can often serve as reflections of our innermost desires, fears, challenges and triumphs. For teenagers, dreams might encompass themes that directly relate to identity, acceptance, societal views and personal journey. The following guided prompts aim to help you navigate and interpret dreams that resonate with your experiences.

Before diving into the interpretation, create a calming environment. Sit comfortably, take deep breaths and recall the dream as vividly as possible. It's essential to approach dream interpretation with an open mind and heart.

Themes of Acceptance

Did the dream involve feelings or situations of acceptance or rejection? Consider the contexts. Were they self-acceptance, societal, familial or in relationships?

Colors and Emotions

Were there any specific colors that stood out in your dream? Colors can often represent emotions. .

Characters and Relationships

Who were the primary characters in the dream? Were they representations of your real-life relationships or symbolic figures? What roles did they play in the dream's narrative?

Closeted Feelings

Were there elements of concealment or revelation in the dream? For instance, hiding in a place or coming out to someone. What emotions did these situations evoke?

Symbols and Significance

Are there symbols, themes, or motifs in the dream that relate to your identity or experiences? Reflect on their potential significance.

Transitions and Transformations

Did you or other characters undergo any transformation in the dream? This could be symbolic of personal growth, transitioning or evolving self-identity.

Conflict and Resolution

Were there conflicts in the dream? How were they resolved? This might hint at inner tensions or external challenges you're facing or have faced.

Symbols of Liberation

Were there moments or symbols of freedom, flight or liberation? How did they make you feel?

Contextual Environments

Consider the setting of the dream. Was it a familiar place, a past environment or somewhere entirely unknown? Environments can reflect current mental and emotional states or past experiences.

Messages or Lessons

Were there clear messages, lessons or advice given in the dream? Who provided them, and how did they relate to your journey?

Remember, dream interpretation is subjective. While these prompts provide a direction, your feelings, intuition and personal experiences play a crucial role in understanding the dream's significance. Embrace the journey of self-exploration and insight that dreams can offer.

Create an artwork or visual representation of a recent dream or a vivid memory that relates to your unconscious.

Repressed Desires

EMBRACING REPRESSED DESIRES

Think of a desire or goal you've hesitated to pursue. What has held you back?

Describe an instance when you felt a strong desire but didn't act on it. What stopped you?

Reflect on your hidden talents or interests that you haven't explored. What might be stopping you from embracing them?

Write about a time when you suppressed your emotions or desires to conform to social expectations.

How do you feel about the idea of acknowledging and embracing
your repressed desires?

*To confront a person with their
own shadow is to show them
their own light.*

-Carl Jung

Make a list of
desires you've
never pursued.
Choose one to take
a small step
toward fulfilling.

Experiment with a
creative hobby or
activity that aligns
with a repressed
desire.

Create a vision
board that
represents your
unfulfilled desires
and goals.

UNPURSUED DESIRES

♡ _______________________________

♡ _______________________________

♡ _______________________________

♡ _______________________________

♡ _______________________________

♡ _______________________________

♡ _______________________________

♡ _______________________________

♡ _______________________________

♡ _______________________________

♡ _______________________________

♡ _______________________________

♡ _______________________________

♡ _______________________________

♡ _______________________________

Make a list of desires you've never pursued. Choose one to take a small step toward fulfilling.

Create a vision board that represents your unfulfilled desires and goals.

Projection

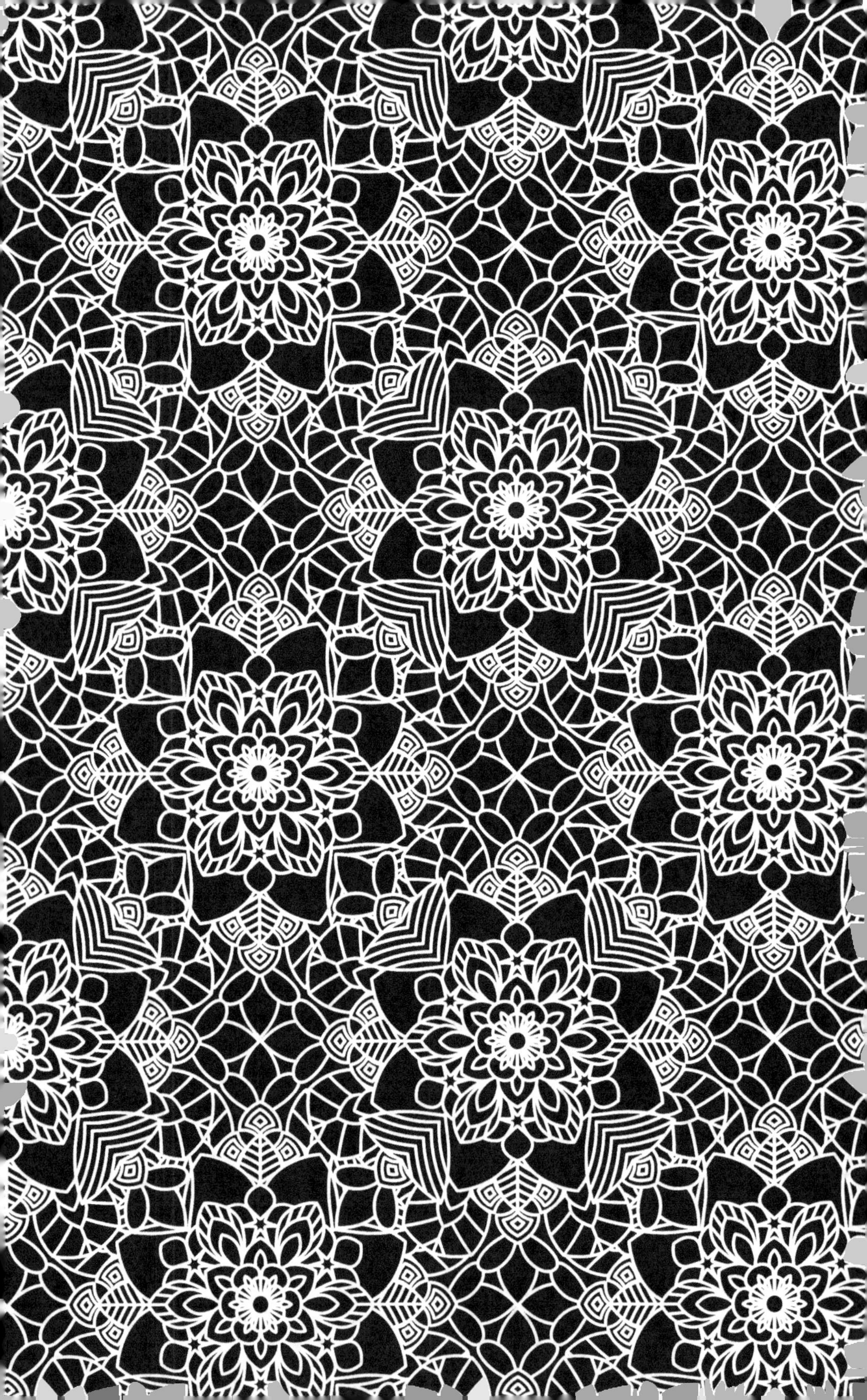

UNDERSTANDING PROJECTION

Recall a recent conflict or disagreement with someone. What emotions did you experience during the conflict?

Describe a situation where you made assumptions about someone's intentions. How might you have projected your own feelings onto them?

Write about a time when you judged someone harshly. Could your judgments be projections of your own fears or insecurities?

Reflect on your relationships. Are there patterns of projection or misinterpretation that you notice?

How do you feel about exploring the concept of projection and its impact on relationships?

We do not see things as they are; we see them as we are.

Anais Nin

Practice active listening in your conversations with others. Pay attention to your reactions and possible projections.

Create a list of affirmations that counteract common negative projections or judgments you make about yourself.

Journal about a challenging relationship and identify moments of projection. How can you address them constructively?

Create a list of affirmations that counteract common negative projections or judgments you make about yourself.

Integration

INTEGRATING YOUR SHADOW

Identify a trait or quality in yourself that you've denied or rejected. How might embracing it bring balance to your life?

Describe a situation where you acted out a hidden aspect of your personality. What did you learn from that experience?

Reflect on a time when you felt a strong internal conflict. What aspects of your shadow were in play?

Write about a positive quality in someone you admire. How might that quality be a reflection of an unacknowledged part of yourself?

How do you feel about the idea of integrating your shadow for personal growth?

Create a "Shadow Self" collage or artwork that represents aspects of yourself you've overlooked or disowned.

Write a letter to yourself from the perspective of an integrated self, offering guidance and support.

Explore a new hobby or activity that aligns with a repressed aspect of your personality

Create a "Shadow Self" collage or artwork that represents
aspects of yourself you've overlooked or disowned.

Integrating Your Shadow

Write a letter to yourself from the perspective of an integrated self, offering guidance and support.

Individuation

EMBARKING ON YOUR INDIVIDUATION JOURNEY

Reflect on your unique strengths, talents, and interests. How can you use them to shape your future?

Describe a moment when you felt completely authentic and true to yourself. What were the circumstances, and how did it feel?

Write about a role model or mentor who inspires you. What qualities do they possess that you admire and aspire to develop?

Explore your long-term goals and aspirations. How can your individuation journey align with these goals?

How do you envision your path of individuation, and what excites you about it?

Individuation does not shut one out from the world but gathers the world to oneself.

-Carl Jung

Create a vision board or timeline of your life goals, both short-term and long-term.

Interview someone you admire and ask them about their journey of self-discovery and personal growth.

Start a project or hobby that allows you to express your unique talents and interests.

Create a vision board or timeline of your life goals, both short-term and long-term.

Moral Ambiguity

NAVIGATING MORAL AMBIGUITY

Recall a situation where you faced a moral dilemma. How did you make your decision, and what values guided you?

Describe a time when you questioned the ethical actions of someone you know. How did it impact your relationship with them?

Reflect on your personal values and ethics. How have they evolved over time, and what has influenced those changes?

Write about a current societal issue that raises moral questions for you. What factors contribute to your stance on the issue?

How do you feel about exploring the concept of moral ambiguity and its role in shadow work?

Good does not become better by being exaggerated, but worse, and a small evil becomes a big one through being disregarded and repressed.

-Carl Jung

Engage in ethical debates or discussions with peers or mentors, exploring different viewpoints on moral issues.

Write a personal code of ethics that reflects your values and principles. Revise it as needed to align with your evolving beliefs.

Explore volunteer or community service opportunities that challenge your ethical perspectives and provide opportunities for growth.

Navigating Moral Ambiguity

Write a personal code of ethics that reflects your values and principles. Revise it as needed to align with your evolving beliefs.

Encounter with the Self

THE ENCOUNTER WITH YOUR TRUE SELF

Describe a moment when you felt a deep sense of self-acceptance and authenticity. What led to this experience?

Reflect on the people and experiences that have shaped your self-identity. How have they influenced your perception of your true self?

Write about your dreams and aspirations. How do they align with your authentic self, and what steps can you take to pursue them?

Explore your core values and principles. How do they resonate with your true self, and how can you honor them in your life?

How do you feel about the idea of encountering your true self through shadow work?

Your time is limited, don't waste it living someone else's life.

-Steve Jobs

Write a letter to your future self, envisioning the person you aspire to become and the authentic life you aim to lead.

Engage in mindfulness or meditation practices that help you connect with your innermost self and reduce external influences.

Share your authentic self with a trusted friend or mentor through a candid conversation.

The Encounter with Your True Self

Write a letter to your future self, envisioning the person you aspire to become and the authentic life you aim to lead.

DAILY MINDFULNESS EXERCISES

"*In each of us there is another whom we do not know.*"

-Carl Jung

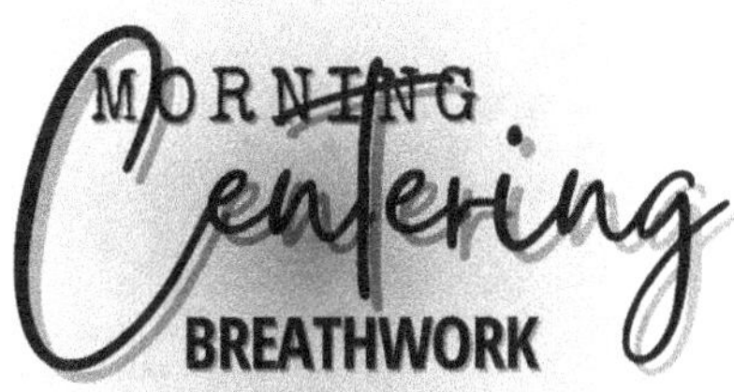

Position

Sit comfortably in a quiet space, spine straight, hands resting on your lap.

Breathe

Inhale deeply through your nose for a count of four.

Hold

Pause and hold the breath for a count of four.

Exhale

Slowly release the breath through the mouth for a count of six.

Reflect

Do this cycle five times. With each breath, visualize yourself letting go of any anxiety and drawing in positive energy.

Pause

Find a quiet moment during your day.

List

Think of three things you're grateful for related to your journey.

Acknowledge

Recognize the growth and understanding that has come from these experiences.

"*Enjoy the little things, for one day you may look back and realize they were the big things.*"

-Robert Brault

When feeling overwhelmed:

See

Look around and name five things you can see.

Touch

Acknowledge four items you can touch or feel.

Hear

Listen carefully and identify three sounds.

Smell

Recognize two scents around you.

Taste

Acknowledge one taste, perhaps by having a sip of water or a snack.

Transformation

EMBRACING TRANSFORMATION

Reflect on a significant personal transformation you've experienced. How did it impact your life and relationships?

Describe a challenge or adversity you faced that ultimately led to personal growth. What did you learn from overcoming it?

Write about the changes you hope to see in yourself as a result of your shadow work journey. What are your transformational goals?

Explore the idea of embracing change as a constant in life. How can you adapt and grow through various life transitions?

- How do you feel about the idea of embracing transformation as a result of your shadow work?

I must be willing to give up what I am in order to become what I will be.

-Albert Einstein

Set specific, achievable goals for your personal growth and outline the steps to work toward them.

Create a transformation journal to document your progress, insights, and moments of personal growth throughout your journey.

Seek out mentors or role models who have undergone significant transformations and learn from their experiences.

WHEEL *of* LIFE

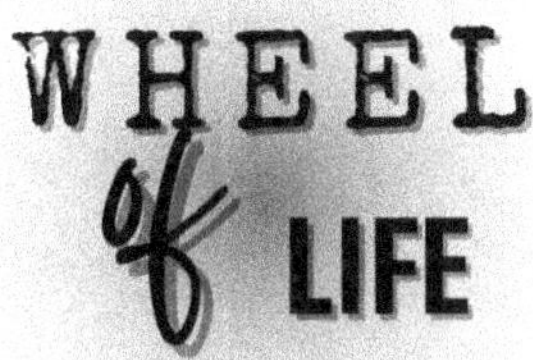

The wheel of life is a great tool that helps you better understand what you can do to make your life more balanced. Think about the 8 life categories below, and rate them from 1 - 10.

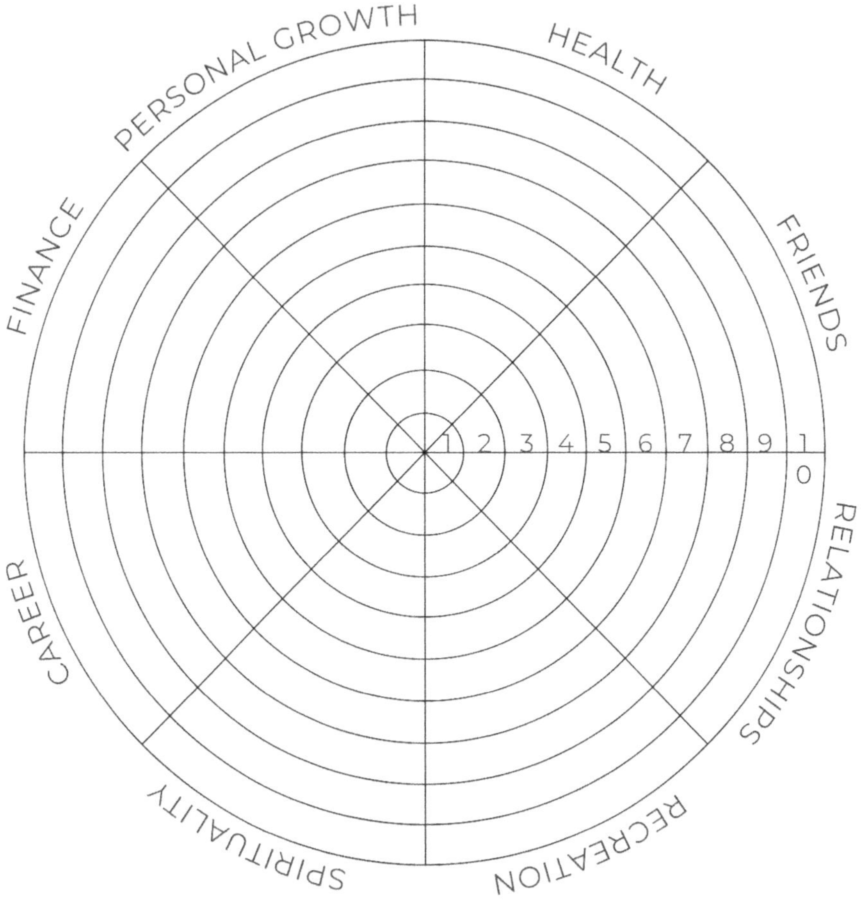

When setting goals, make sure it follows the SMART structure. Use the questions below to create your goals.

S	SPECIFIC — WHAT DO I WANT TO ACCOMPLISH?	
M	MEASURABLE — HOW WILL I KNOW WHEN IT IS ACCOMPLISHED?	
A	ACHIEVABLE — HOW CAN THE GOAL BE ACCOMPLISHED?	
R	RELEVANT — DOES THIS SEEM WORTHWHILE?	
T	TIME BOUND — WHEN CAN I ACCOMPLISH THIS GOAL?	

For each of the categories below, write down things you are doing well and where you need improvement. Take the time to reflect on these, and write a goal for each category.

CATEGORY	WHAT I'M DOING WELL	WHERE I NEED IMPROVEMENT	MY GOALS
FAMILY			
FRIENDS			
WORK/ SCHOOL			
BODY			
MENTAL HEALTH			
SPIRITUALITY			

SMART GOALS

Outline your SMART goals

GOAL	START DATE:	DUE DATE:

GOAL PROGRESS: 0%   ☐☐☐☐☐☐☐☐☐☐   100%

ACTION STEPS	POSSIBLE OBSTACLES

HOW TO OVERCOME OBSTACLES

MILESTONE LOGS

- **Date:** When did this milestone occur?

- **Description:** Describe the event or realization.

- **Feelings:** What emotions did you experience?

- **Impact:** How did this milestone shape or influence your journey?

Date:

Description:

Feelings:

Impact:

Create a transformation journal to document your progress, insights, and moments of personal growth throughout your journey.

Date:

Description:

Feelings:

Impact:

Date:

Description:

Feelings:

Impact:

Date:

Description:

Feelings:

Impact:

Date:

Description:

Feelings:

Impact:

Date:

Description:

Feelings:

Impact:

Date:

Description:

Feelings:

Impact:

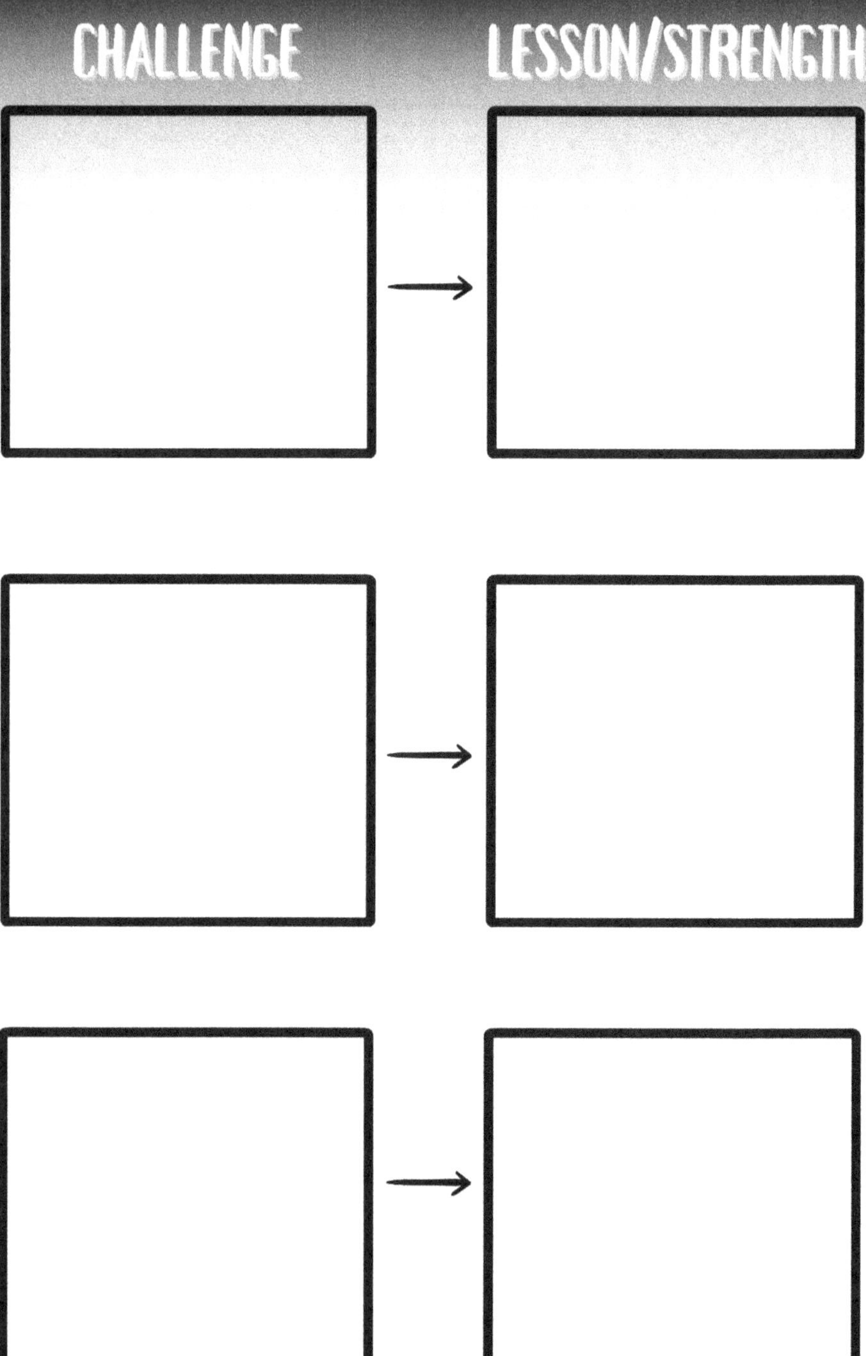

It's essential to pause and express gratitude for the journey, even for the difficult moments, as they've shaped who you are today. List 5 challenges you've faced. Next to each, note a lesson or strength that came out of that challenge.

BONUS

- Gratitude Jar
- Mirror Talk
- Emotional Check-ins
- Five Word Reflection
- Identifying Archetypes
- Strengths and Shadows
- Negative Beliefs and Positive Affirmations
- Symbols and Their Meanings

THE *Gratitude* JAR

Daily or weekly, jot down things you're grateful for that relate to your journey.

Spend a few minutes each day talking positively to yourself in front of a mirror, reaffirming your worth and identity.

EMOTIONAL CHECK-INS

Emotional check-ins serve as touchpoints, allowing you to gauge and understand your emotional state at different times. This practice encourages self-awareness, validation of feelings and recognition of patterns.

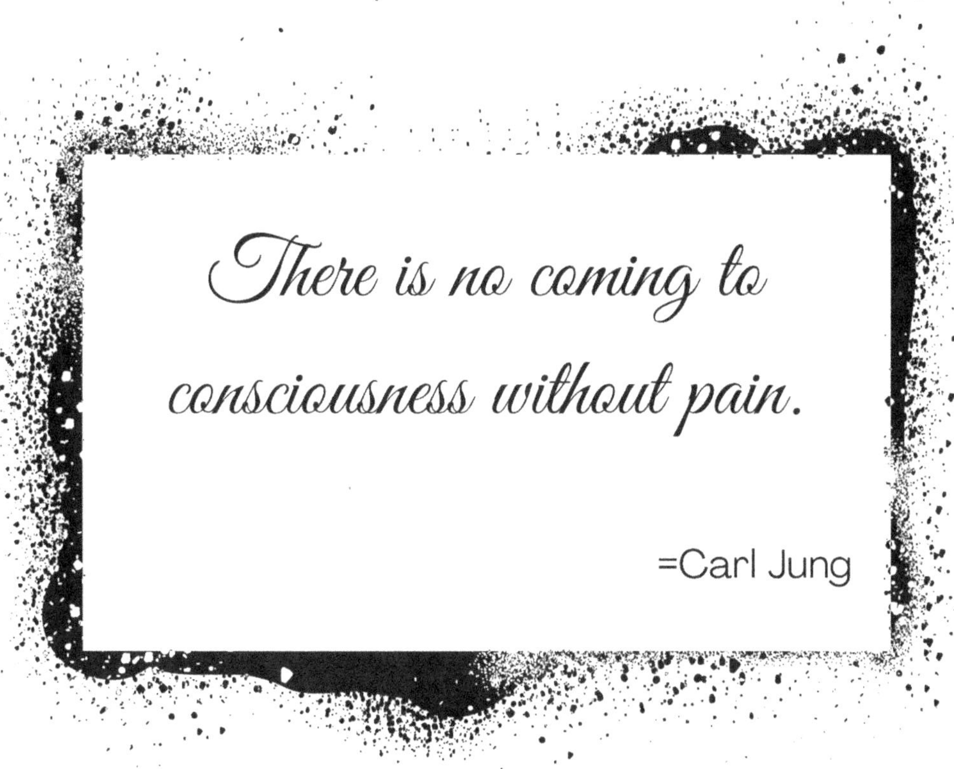

Regularly tuning into your emotions helps in understanding yourself better, making informed decisions and fostering a deep connection with your inner self. Over time, these emotional check-ins can serve as a guidepost, helping you navigate through life's challenges and joys with resilience and authenticity.

DAILY EMOTIONAL LOG

Current Emotional State
Describe in one word.

Physical Sensations
Any tension, relaxation or peculiar sensations in the body?

Accompanying Thoughts
What's on your mind that might be influencing this emotion?

Possible Trigger
Was there an event, comment, interaction or memory that sparked this emotion?

Needs & Wants
What do you need or want right now to support this emotion or shift it?

Affirmation
Write a positive teaching-related affirmation.

WEEKLY EMOTIONAL REFLECTION

Most Recurring Emotion

Which emotion appeared the most this week?

Proudest Moment

A highlight from your week.

Challenging Emotional Moment

Which situation was emotionally challenging?

Self-Care Actions

List 3 things you did this week to take care of your emotional well-being.

Intentions for Next Week

Set 1-2 emotional or mental health intentions for the coming week.

"Until you make the unconscious conscious, it will direct your life and you will call it fate."

Carl Jung

MONTHLY EMOTIONAL OVERVIEW

Emotional High
Which day or event was a high point, emotionally speaking and why?

Emotional Low
Which day or event was challenging, and what did you learn from it?

Support System
Who supported you emotionally this month, and how?

Gratitude
List 3 emotional or personal growth moments you're grateful for this month.

Looking Ahead
One goal or intention for your emotional well-being for the upcoming month.

"Emotion is the chief source of all becoming-conscious. There can be no transforming of darkness into light and of apathy into movement without emotion."

Carl Jung

With caution, ask close friends or family to describe you in five words. Reflect on these words and how they make you feel about yourself. Remember, this is just an external viewpoint and does not define your entirety.

IDENTIFYING ARCHETYPES

Carl Jung identified several archetypes in his theory of the collective unconscious. Some of the key archetypes he described include:

- **The Persona:** This is the social mask or facade that individuals present to the outside world. It represents the way we want to be seen by others.
- **The Shadow:** The shadow represents the unconscious, darker aspects of ourselves that we may not be aware of or may try to repress. It includes our fears, insecurities, and hidden desires.
- **The Anima and Animus:** These are the inner aspects of the opposite gender within each person. The anima represents the feminine qualities within males, while the animus represents the masculine qualities within females.
- **The Self:** The self is the central and most important archetype, representing the unity and integration of the individual's personality. It represents the striving for wholeness and self-realization.
- **The Hero:** The hero archetype embodies the qualities of courage, strength, and the willingness to face challenges and overcome obstacles. It represents the quest for personal growth and transformation.
- **The Mother:** The mother archetype represents nurturing, caregiving, and the maternal qualities of love, protection, and sustenance.
- **The Father:** The father archetype embodies authority, guidance, and the paternal qualities of protection, discipline, and wisdom.
- **The Child:** The child archetype symbolizes innocence, potential, and the desire for new beginnings. It represents the creative and playful aspects of the self

- **The Wise Old Man:** This archetype embodies wisdom, knowledge, and guidance. It represents the quest for understanding and the search for meaning in life.
- **The Trickster:** The trickster archetype is characterized by mischief, humor, and a tendency to challenge the status quo. It often represents the need for change and transformation.

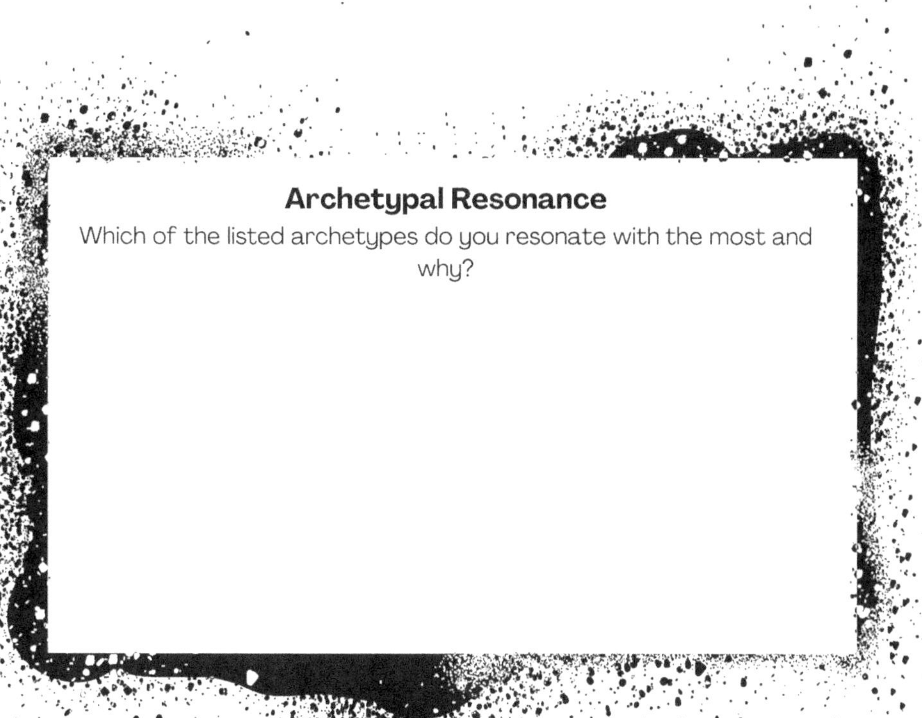

Personal Stories

Share a story or memory where you felt you embodied one of these archetypes.

Future Aspirations

Which archetype do you aspire to become, and what steps can you take to embrace its qualities?

Who do you look up to that represents one of these archetypes?
Why?

> *"It takes courage to grow up and become who you really are."*
>
> -E.E. Cummings

Archetype Role-play

Choose an archetype that intrigues you. Spend a day embodying the qualities of this archetype. Journal about the experience.

For each archetype, create a mood board (using images, quotes, colors, etc.) that you feel best represents its essence.

For each archetype, create a mood board (using images, quotes, colors, etc.) that you feel best represents its essence.

For each archetype, create a mood board (using images, quotes, colors, etc.) that you feel best represents its essence.

For each archetype, create a mood board (using images, quotes, colors, etc.) that you feel best represents its essence.

For each archetype, create a mood board (using images, quotes, colors, etc.) that you feel best represents its essence.

STRENGTHS AND SHADOWS

The duality of our human experience means that with strengths often come shadows — areas of potential pitfalls or challenges that can arise from the same qualities that give us power. Embracing an archetype is not just about harnessing its strengths but also about understanding and navigating its shadows. This section is dedicated to introspecting on both these aspects, aiming to bring about a deeper self-awareness and balance.

Shadows Unveiled

Delve deeper into the potential challenges or pitfalls associated with each archetype. Have you experienced these shadows? How did you handle them?

Balancing Act

Reflect on times when you felt a conflict between the strengths and shadows of an archetype. How did you navigate this balance?

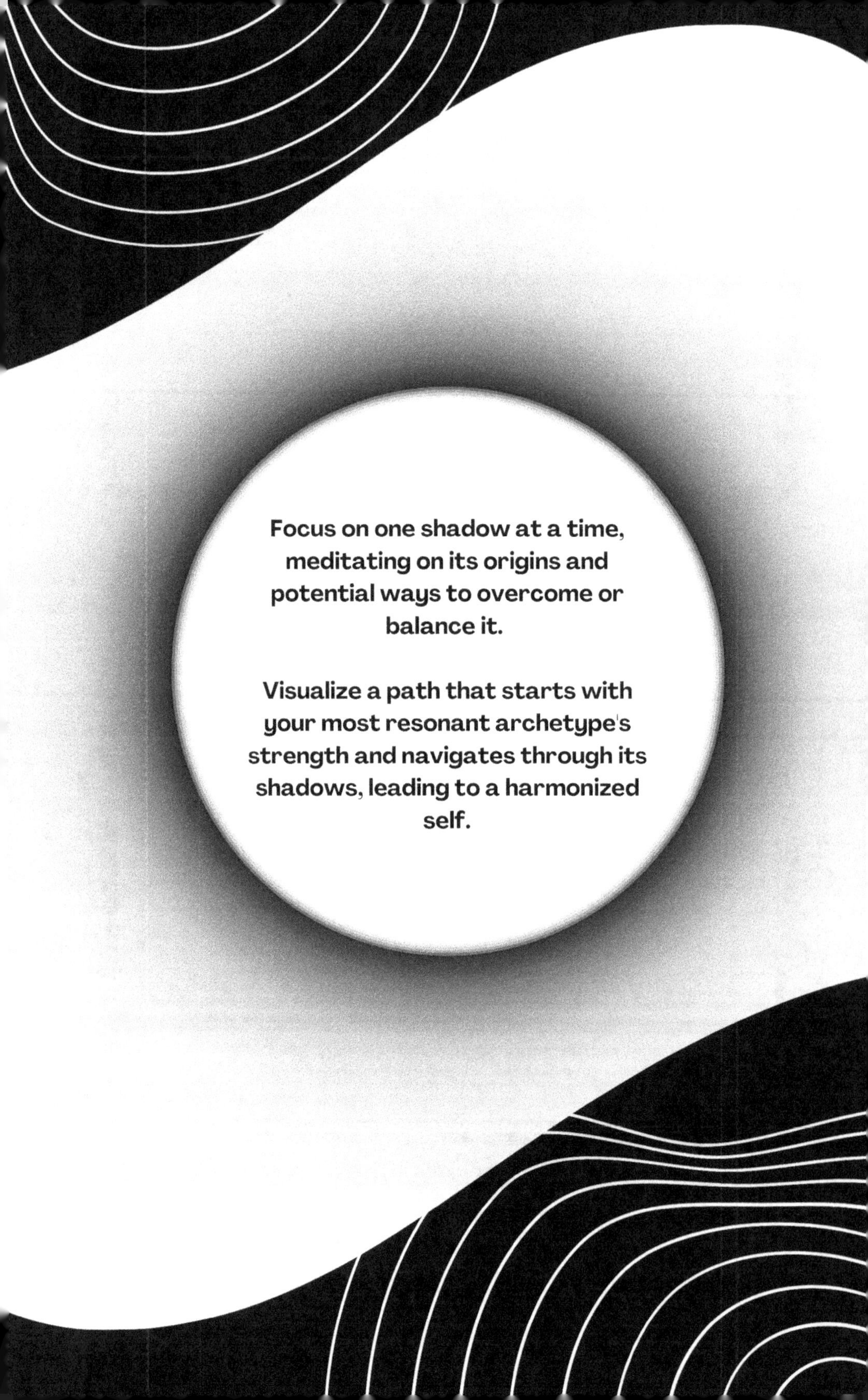

Focus on one shadow at a time,
meditating on its origins and
potential ways to overcome or
balance it.

Visualize a path that starts with
your most resonant archetype's
strength and navigates through its
shadows, leading to a harmonized
self.

Write affirmations based on the strengths of your chosen archetypes. Choose one each day and reflect on it.

STRENGTHS & SHADOWS
DIARY

Dedicate a few pages to each archetype, jotting down daily instances where you exhibited its strengths or encountered its shadows.

Diving into the depths of strengths and shadows offers a holistic understanding of each archetype and, by extension, ourselves. This reflection helps in harnessing the full potential of each archetype, allowing us to grow and evolve in our unique journeys. Remember, shadows are not to be feared but understood and integrated.

In all chaos, there is a cosmos, in all disorder, a secret order. Strengths and shadows are not enemies but two sides of the same coin, and the path to wholeness requires embracing both.

-Carl Jung

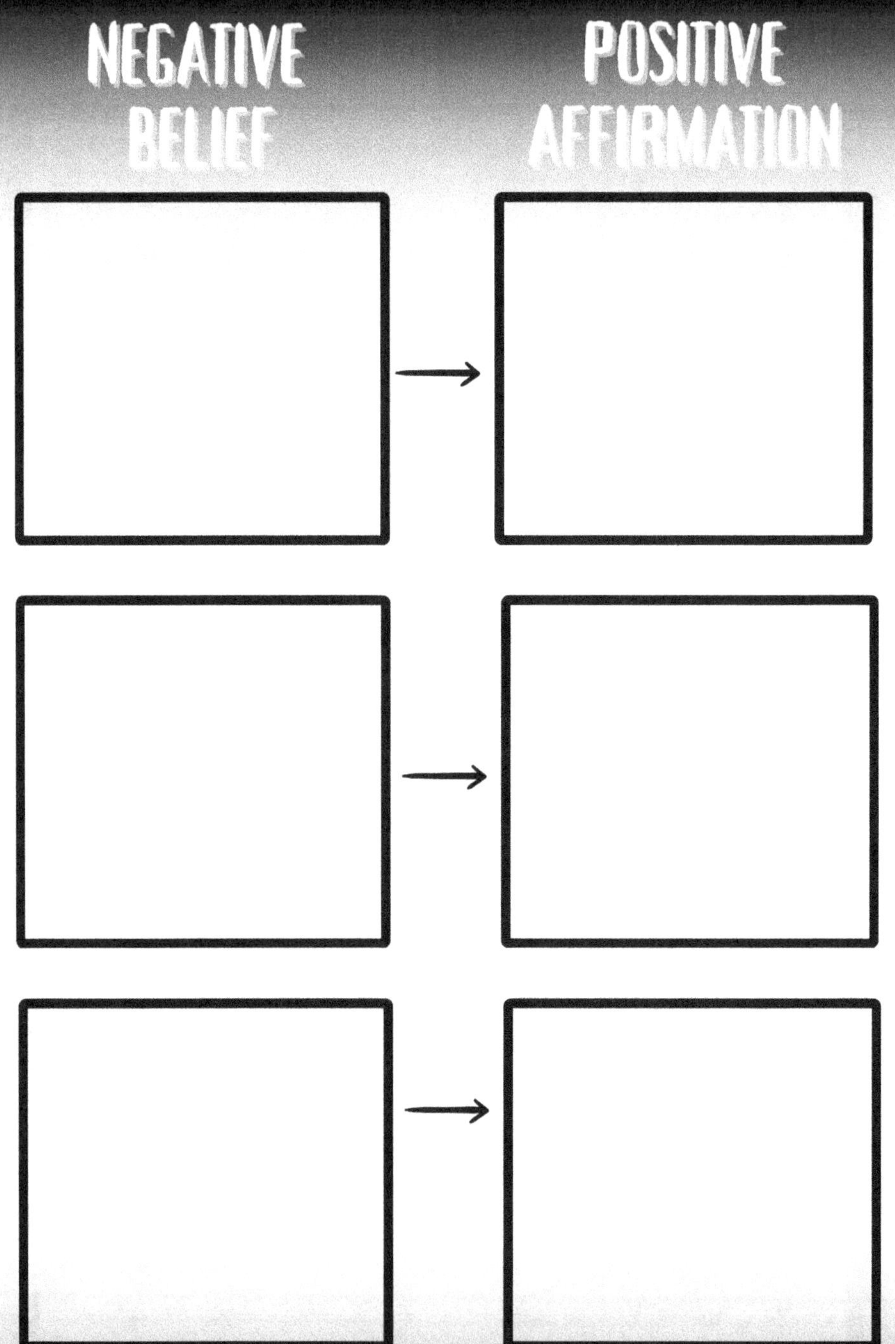

List down the negative beliefs or feelings you have internalized. For each, try to counteract it with a positive affirmation or truth about yourself.

SYMBOLS AND THEIR MEANINGS

In the context of Jungian psychology and shadow work, symbols often appear in dreams, fantasies, or even in everyday life. These symbols can hold deep personal meaning and may offer insights into one's unconscious and the process of self-discovery. Here are some common symbols that teens might encounter and their potential meanings in the context of shadow work:

- **Dark or Shadowy Figures:** Seeing dark or shadowy figures in dreams or fantasies can represent the presence of the shadow self, the hidden and repressed aspects of one's personality. It may be an invitation to explore these hidden traits and integrate them.
- **Masks:** Masks can symbolize the persona, the social facade that individuals present to the world. Finding or wearing a mask in a dream might indicate a desire to explore one's true identity beneath the mask.
- **Animals:** Different animals can have various symbolic meanings. For example, a snake might represent hidden desires or fears, while a bird could symbolize freedom or spirituality. The specific animal and its actions in the dream can provide additional insights.
- **Water:** Water often represents emotions and the unconscious mind. The state of the water (calm, turbulent, murky) can offer clues about one's emotional state and the need to explore and navigate these feelings.
- **Labyrinths or Mazes:** These symbols can represent the complexity of the psyche and the journey of self-discovery. Navigating a labyrinth might symbolize the process of exploring one's inner world.
- **Keys:** Finding or using keys in dreams can represent unlocking hidden aspects of the self or gaining access to new insights and self-awareness.
- **Mirrors:** Mirrors can symbolize self-reflection and self-awareness. Seeing a distorted reflection might indicate a need to confront distorted self-perceptions.
- **Monsters or Creatures:** Imaginary creatures or monsters can represent inner fears, anxieties, or unresolved conflicts. Confronting or taming these creatures can symbolize the process of facing and integrating one's fears.
- **Journey or Travel:** Embarking on a journey, whether in a dream or a symbolic representation, often signifies

personal growth and transformation. It can represent the quest for self-discovery and individuation.

- **Death and Rebirth:** Symbolic deaths and rebirths can represent the process of shedding old beliefs, habits, or identities to make way for personal growth and transformation.

"*Symbols, by their very nature, can so unite opposites that these no longer diverge or conflict, but mutually supplement one another and give meaningful shape to life.*"

Carl Jung

Draw, print or paste pictures of symbols. Next to each, jot down its known historical or cultural significance and any personal connections or feelings you associate with it.

Personal Resonance

Is there a particular symbol that deeply resonates with you? Why do you feel a connection to this symbol?

Symbol Evolution

How have you observed the evolution or change in the meaning and use of any of these symbols over time?

Creating Your Symbol

If you were to design a symbol that captures your personal journey, what would it look like? Sketch or describe it.

Symbols in Everyday Life

For one week, pay attention to the use of symbols around you, whether it's in advertising, during a parade, on social media, etc.

Note down:

- The symbol you observed.
- The context in which it was displayed.
- Your initial reaction and feelings towards its use in that particular context.

Symbols often serve as anchors or reminders. They can uplift, motivate and connect us to a broader community. In this section, consider how these symbols can be integrated into your daily life as sources of strength, pride and unity.

It's essential to remember that the meaning of symbols in shadow work is highly personal and can vary from one individual to another. Approach these symbols with curiosity and explore your own unique interpretations and associations.

COINCIDENCES WITH MEANING

Synchronicity, a term coined by Carl Jung, refers to meaningful coincidences that seem to have a deeper, often personal significance. These coincidences can often serve as affirmations, guideposts or signals from the universe, especially during times of self-discovery, acceptance or advocacy.

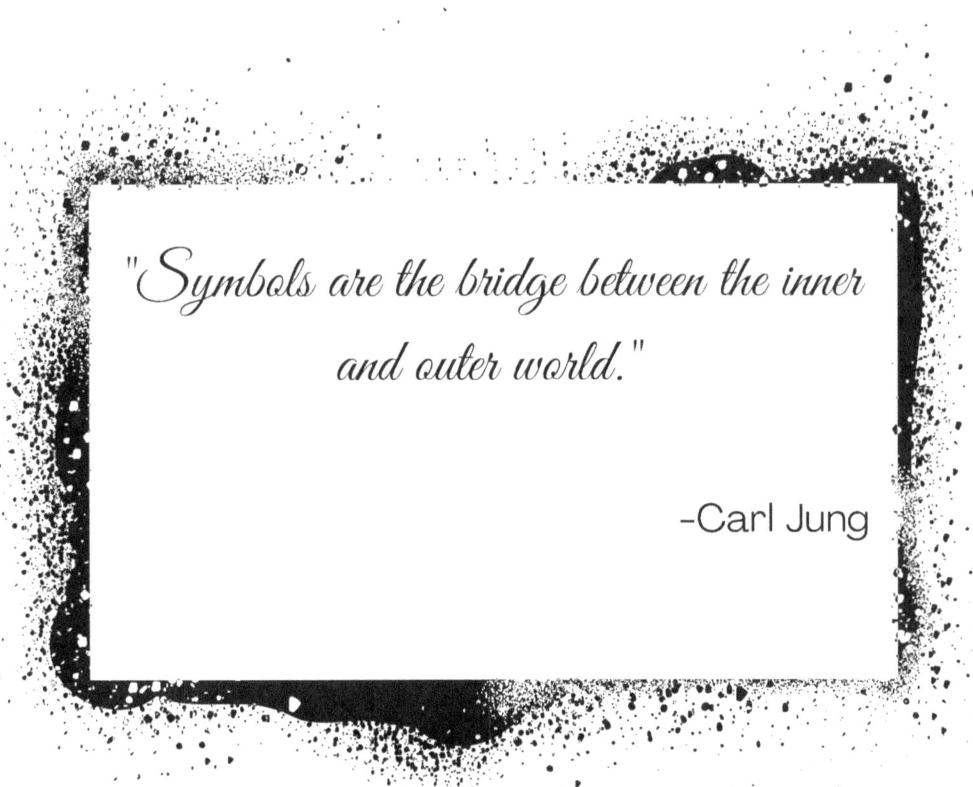

COINCIDENCE LOG

Date & Time
When did this event happen?

Description
Detail the synchronistic event.

Feelings
How did you feel when it
happened?

Personal Significance
Why do you feel this event was more than just a random occurrence? What
deeper meaning or connection might it have for you?

Date & Time:

Description:

Feelings:

Personal Significance:

COINCIDENCE LOG

Date & Time

Description

Feelings

Personal Significance

Date & Time:

Description:

Feelings:

Personal Significance:

Patterns

Have you noticed any recurring themes or patterns in the synchronicities you've experienced?

Emotional State

Were there specific emotional states (e.g., feeling lost, hopeful or in need of guidance) that preceded these synchronistic events?

Messages

If the universe was trying to send you a message through these events, what do you think it might be?

"The symbol is a living body, animated by the energy that goes through it."

-Carl Jung

REFLECTION ON PAST SYNCHRONICITIES

Think about a meaningful coincidence from your past that had a significant impact on your journey, such as meeting a person who became a mentor or stumbling upon a community event that felt like 'home.'

The Event

Describe this past synchronistic event.

The Impact

How did it shape or influence your journey?

Looking Back

With hindsight, do you perceive the event differently now than when it happened?

SEEKING SYNCHRONICITY

Personal growth is a unique and often intense journey. Every step, whether filled with clarity or confusion, contributes to the vibrant spectrum of one's identity. This section is dedicated to acknowledging, celebrating and understanding these milestones.

For one week, become more attuned to the universe's whispers. Each evening, reflect on the day and note down:

- Any coincidences, no matter how small.
- Your emotional state before they occurred.
- Possible meanings or messages these events might be conveying.

Reflect on how these meaningful coincidences can be seen as forms of support or guidance, especially during challenging moments or crossroads in your journey. How can recognizing and valuing these synchronicities bolster your sense of connection, direction and hope?

CONCLUSION
Your Ongoing Shadow Journey

Congratulations on completing this transformative journey of self-discovery and personal growth through the Shadow Work Journal for Teens. You've ventured into the depths of your psyche, confronted hidden aspects of yourself, and embraced the power of your shadow. This journey marks just the beginning of a lifelong path toward authenticity and self-realization.

As you reflect on the pages you've filled and the insights you've gained, remember that shadow work is not a one-time endeavor but an ongoing exploration. The shadows within you are not to be feared but understood, accepted, and integrated. By continuing to shine a light on your hidden aspects, you will uncover even more treasures of self-awareness and personal growth.

Your shadow journey has equipped you with valuable tools—self-reflection, self-compassion, and self-empowerment—that will serve you well as you navigate the complexities of adolescence and beyond. The challenges you face and the victories you celebrate are all part of the rich tapestry of your personal growth.

Embrace your uniqueness, for it is your strengths and your shadows that make you who you are. Remember that there is no one-size-fits-all path to self-discovery. Trust your inner wisdom, stay curious, and continue to explore the depths of your own psyche.

Your authentic self is a radiant light waiting to shine brightly in the world. As you continue your shadow journey, may you grow in self-acceptance, cultivate healthier relationships, and become the hero of your own story. The adventure of a lifetime awaits you—embrace it with an open heart and an unquenchable thirst for self-discovery.

Thank you for allowing the Shadow Work Journal for Teens to be a part of your transformative journey. Keep journaling, keep exploring, and keep shining your light. Your authentic self is a beautiful work in progress, and the world is a better place with you in it.

THANK YOU

for getting this book and for making it all the way to the end!

Before you go, I wanted to ask you for one small favor. Could you please consider posting a review? Because posting a review is the best and easiest way to support the work of independent authors like me.

Your feedback will help me a ton!

Also By Callie Parker

The Ultimate Self-Help Narcissistic Abuse Recovery Book

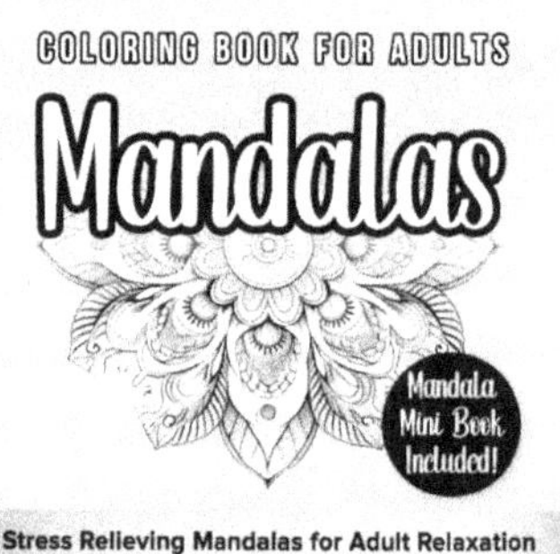

ADHD VS. YOU
Owning the Chaos and Making It Your B*tch

Coloring Book for Adults
Mandalas

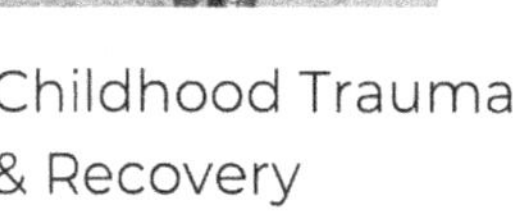

Childhood Trauma
& Recovery
Healing Your Inner Child

Childhood Trauma &
Recovery Workbook
Healing Your Inner Child

The Shadow Work Journal Series

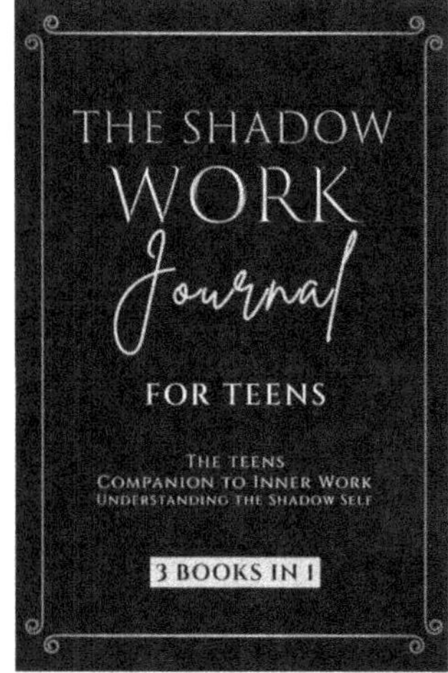

The Shadow Work
Journal
for Couples

The Shadow Work
Journal
for Teens

The Shadow Work
Journal
LGBTQ+ Edition

Microdosing
Through
Your Shadow Work